12

Puppy Kindergarten

Miriam Fields-Babineau

Photo Credits: Isabelle Francais, Robert Pearcy

© T.F.H. Publications, Inc.

Distributed in the UNITED STATES to the Pet Trade by T.F.H. Publications, Inc., 1 TFH Plaza, Neptune City, NJ 07753; on the Internet at www.tfh.com; in CANADA by Rolf C. Hagen Inc., 3225 Sartelon St., Montreal, Quebec H4R 1E8; Pet Trade by H & L Pet Supplies Inc., 27 Kingston Crescent, Kitchener, Ontario N2B 2T6; in ENGLAND by T.F.H. Publications, PO Box 74, Havant PO9 5TT; in AUSTRALIA AND THE SOUTH PACIFIC by T.F.H. (Australia), Pty. Ltd., Box 149, Brookvale 2100 N.S.W., Australia; in NEW ZEALAND by Brooklands Aquarium Ltd., 5 McGiven Drive, New Plymouth, RD1 New Zealand; in SOUTH AFRICA by Rolf C. Hagen S.A. (PTY.) LTD., P.O. Box 201199, Durban North 4016, South Africa; in Japan by T.F.H. Publications. Published by T.F.H. Publications, Inc.

MANUFACTURED IN THE
UNITED STATES OF AMERICA
BY T.F.H. PUBLICATIONS, INC.

Table of Contents

Introduction to Puppy Kindergarten

Puppies are cute, fun, and very special. Although they are quite infantile, their brains are fully developed. Puppies can learn anything that an adult dog can learn. The only difference is that due to their tender age, their attention span and work tolerance is very short. However, this does not get in the way of their learning. Their minds are like sponges, ready to soak up their surroundings. In fact, puppies strive to learn new things.

Puppies can easily adapt to new training methods, because their behavioral patterns have not yet been set.

Puppies have the ability to learn anything that an adult dog can learn. However, they have short attention spans and need to move at a slower pace.

The best thing about training puppies is that they want to learn. Their behaviors are not yet set, which makes them more open to forming proper behavior patterns. Teaching a two-month-old pup will be far easier than teaching a five-month-old pup. The younger pup only wants to please, whereas the older pup has already learned bad habits that must be corrected. It is less difficult to mold a dog into a well-behaved pet than to overcome bad habits while trying to teach at the same time.

Puppy kindergarten can help you mold your puppy into the perfect dog. With the help of play training, patience, and lots of love, your pup will do anything you want, whenever you want. The only stipulation is that you must start now and not later when your puppy begins behaving in an annoying manner.

At the age of two months, your puppy is able to learn

By two months of age, puppies should be able to respond to the basic commands.

Introducing new things, like the leash, to your puppy in a gradual manner will help him adjust more easily as well as make his associations with a leash and collar positive.

how to come, sit, lie down, and walk with you for short distances. He is capable of learning where to go potty, what he can and cannot put his mouth on, where to sleep and eat, and more. By three months of age, his brain is fully developed, and he can learn to heel and stay. He can even learn to identify toys, other animals, and people by name.

If you start training your puppy at two months of age, you will not experience the worst stage in puppy adolescence, which occurs between five and eight months. When your pup reaches six months of age, he'll know the house rules and listen when you tell him to do something. He will not be destructive or neurotic. In fact, you'll be on your way to a great, long-term relationship with your puppy.

PUPPY DEVELOPMENT

There are three distinct periods in puppy development. The first is the social

development period, which occurs between the ages of 6 to 12 weeks. At this time, your puppy is learning about new people and environments. This is the best time to move him away from the comfort of his littermates into a new home. He will be more accepting and easily influenced by his new family pack. Your pup will appear to be very dependent on you. When you go somewhere, he will naturally follow. When frightened, he will hide behind your legs. Your puppy will only learn to accept new things if you are there with him. In this stage, he is very dependent on pack unity. This is the best time to begin training him because he is looking to you for guidance.

The second stage is the fear imprint period, which can occur at four months and again at nine months of age. At this time, everything can be scary. Make certain that your puppy is never forced to confront something that frightens him. Always coax and coerce him with the use of praise or food. This will turn a bad situation into something positive.

For example, if you put a leash on him and try walking him around, he'll pull back and yipe, because he does not understand what you want. This will instill a bad impression in his brain, and he'll always pull away from you when he sees the leash. Using the puppy kindergarten techniques while teaching your pup to heel will ensure

Providing your puppy with the proper training at an early age will enable him to become a well-behaved and obedient adult dog.

At four to five months of age, puppies begin to test their newfound independence as well as the boundaries set by their owners.

that he has positive associations with the leash.

At four to five months of age, your puppy will become more independent. He will test his environment to learn what will and will not be tolerated. He will also be very persistent about trying to do things his way. Many pups tend to be very mouthy at this age, and those that are dominant may exhibit aggressive behavior when things don't go as they wish. Training your pup at this age can be very frustrating. However, if you start training him at two months, you can easily control these outbursts in a manner that your pup will understand.

The third stage of development is adolescence. What once was a well-behaved puppy that was eager to please you will turn into a rambunctious, assertive dog

Although your puppy may tend to get mouthy during adolescence, remain consistent and firm in your training to achieve the best possible results.

that ignores your commands. Your puppy will begin noticing things he had previously ignored, such as other dogs, cats, and squirrels.

Canine adolescence normally begins around five months of age and can last anywhere from the age of ten months to a year and a half. During this period, your puppy's energy level peaks, and he will feel very self-confident and begin to test his boundaries, which include the house rules. The main difference between preadolescence and adolescence is the increase in energy level and persistence. If you had maintained the status quo during preadolescence, your pup may no longer be as mouthy. However, he will still be more easily distracted and more likely to turn a deaf ear on you at times.

If you obtained your pup to be a family pet, you should have him neutered before he exhibits sexually disruptive behaviors. Whether male or female, a dog can be neutered at six to seven months of age. This operation is not traumatic. In most cases, you can pick your pup up the evening of or the morning after the operation. Be responsible and neuter your pet—you will have a well-behaved, more attentive family member.

In addition to neutering, there are other things you can do to make sure that your puppy remains in your good graces and learns the house rules. Exercise is the most important thing you can offer him while his energy level is soaring. If you work during the day, take your puppy on a brisk walk just

It's a good idea to have your puppy sit or lie down before receiving attention. This enforces good behavior and teaches him that he must work for what he wants.

While some pups respond better to food treats, such as freeze-dried liver or cheese, others are more responsive to toys.

before leaving and when you return home. If you remain home during the day, you should set aside exercise time for your pup a few times each day. Go to a park or ball field and let him run. If you know of any friendly dogs in the neighborhood, get in touch with their owners and arrange a time to meet. Your puppy will love nothing better than to play with another dog. This is the best means of wearing down his energy without having to wear yourself out, plus he learns valu-able social skills. After a long run, your puppy will listen better and be more relaxed.

Another thing you should do is to remain consistent and maintain your leadership position. Your puppy will be testing your authority. Do not allow him to misbehave. Make your puppy earn his treats, such as doing a sit or a trick. Have him sit or lie down before he gets his meals. Make him sit before receiving attention. This teaches your pup that he must work for what he wants.

The last thing you should do is give your puppy a treat or attention if he barks at you. The bark is a demand for attention. You should only give him attention when you choose to do so.

Although adolescence will be trying and frustrating, do not give up. In a few more months, your puppy will be a well-behaved family member and you will be able to trust him in the house. Remember that your dog will live to be anywhere from 8 to 17 years old. Every child needs to learn about his environment in order to grow into a responsible adult. Your dog will always be looking for his master's weaknesses. Remain consistent throughout his life, and he'll be a great companion.

PUPPY PERSONALITIES

There are several tests that you can conduct to discover more about your pup's personality, which is very important when planning your training approach and general living conditions. Some pups will respond to your voice, others to food or a toy, and others can be so indifferent that they don't care what you have to offer—they simply ignore you and go off on their own.

Puppy kindergarten works best on puppies that respond to voice, food, or toy rewards. This is a very coercive type of training, and without that ready response, it cannot be utilized. If your pup does not respond to these things, consult with a professional trainer. The last thing you want is to have your puppy learn to avoid his training sessions due to bad experi-

Training a puppy that has a dominant personality can be a challenge. If your puppy is not listening to you, simply look him in the eyes and reprimand him firmly.

This Boxer puppy has done his homework on how to sit properly.

Puppy Kindergarten

This Bullmastiff gets a handshake for a job well done!

ences. There are other ways to train a puppy that does not respond to puppy kindergarten, and a professional trainer will be able to help.

The first evaluation is the touch test. Sit on the floor next to your puppy and gently touch him all over, from his head, ears, and mouth down to his tail and toes. Look in his ears, at his teeth, separate his toes, and lift his tail.

Your puppy's responses may be as follows:
1. He remains still and allows you to touch him.
2. He allows you to touch him but is very wiggly.
3. He shivers at your touch.
4. He bites at your fingers.
5. He bites at your fingers and tries to pull away from you.

The first response, remaining still and allowing you to touch him, is ideal but rarely found in young puppies, because they are always too energetic. If your pup exhibits this behavior, he is very amiable and will be easy to train.

The second response, allowing you to touch him but being wiggly, is the most normal response. Puppies love to be touched but also tend to play with those who touch them. Allow your pup to move around while you examine him. Keep your touch gentle and soothing, which teaches him to enjoy your attention.

The third response, shivering at your touch, exhibits a very fearful puppy. This type of pup will be more difficult to train, and you should consult with a professional trainer. A fearful puppy must be trained only with coercion, which can be time-consuming and requires a lot of patience.

The fourth response, a pup that bites at your fingers but still allows you to touch him, demonstrates a more assertive personality. This pup will still be very likely to respond to puppy kindergarten, but his attention will tend to wander. Be sure to follow through with your commands when he is distracted, which may mean physically moving him into position.

The fifth response, a pup that bites at your fingers and then tries to run off, requires the help of a professional trainer. This pup is dominant and independent. If the reward is attractive enough, he'll probably learn to work for it, but when it comes to behavior modification, you'll need to be assertive and absolutely consistent.

The second test is a combination of teaching your

If your pup has a tendency to bite or nip at your fingers when you touch him, it is likely that he has a more assertive personality. Be firm in your corrections and make him understand that you are the boss.

puppy to target and ensuring that he will work for a reward. Targeting is a means of obtaining your pup's undivided attention. Once you have his attention, you can continue through all the phases of puppy kindergarten without a problem. Targeting is based on the concept of operant conditioning, which means that for each proper response, your pup earns a reward. As your pup learns each portion of an exercise, he is expected to perform more frequently to obtain his reward.

The first step is to discover what your puppy likes. Will he do anything for praise? If so, you can praise him every time he performs well. Most pups will respond well to a treat, such as a piece of freeze-dried liver, cheese, or biscuit, while others prefer a toy, like a ball or a bone. You can test your pup's attention as follows:
1. He hears, smells, or sees the stimulus (reward), and he follows it around.
2. He hears, smells, or sees the stimulus, looks at it, but loses interest.
3. He is exposed to the stimulus, but shows no response.

The first response is optimal. This is a pup that will do anything for that reward. If your pup exhibits the second response, try another type of reward. For example, show your pup a piece of biscuit. He sniffs it but walks away. Instead, try a piece of cheese. Let him have a small piece to garner his interest. If he wants more, you can use the cheese as bait. If not, try the freeze-dried liver.

Here are the steps to teach targeting:

Although sometimes it is inevitable, try to keep your puppy as focused as possible during training sessions. The more he pays attention, the faster he will learn.

1. Hold the bait directly in front of your pup's nose. As soon as he brings his nose closer and touches your hand, praise him and give him the treat. The praise acts as a bridge between your praise and the advent of giving your puppy his treat. Thus, he will learn to look forward to your praise as much as the food or toy reward.
2. Next, place the bait in your hand and let your pup touch his nose to your hand. Praise him, but don't give him the treat. First, move your hand a little to the left. When your pup's nose follows your hand, praise him, and move your hand a little to the right. As soon as his nose moves again with your hand, praise and give him his reward. He is now targeting on your hand.

A pup that shows no response to any type of reward will be far more difficult to train and may not respond easily to the puppy kindergarten approach. A different training procedure will be necessary. However, you may want to try either waiting until he is very hungry, such as at mealtime, or offer a different selection of rewards. There are very few dogs that will not respond to

Praise plays a very important role in your puppy's training regimen and behavior. Make sure that you consistently provide him with positive reinforcement.

some type of food or toy.

The third test is an evaluation of the distraction threshold of your puppy. This is important, because the more your puppy pays attention, the faster he will learn. If he looks at what is going on around him, he will be far more difficult to train. This is a very difficult test, because all puppies are easily distracted.

While you are working on targeting, have someone drop a set of keys, a book, or some other item that makes a light noise. Following are some possible reactions:
1. The puppy ignores the distraction and continues to target.
2. The puppy glances at the distraction and returns to his target.
3. The puppy scoots away from the noise, discovers the cause, and then examines the distraction, eventually returning to target.
4. The puppy goes after the distraction and forgets about targeting altogether.

If your puppy ignores the distraction altogether, you have a great working dog. If he glances at the distraction but returns to targeting, you still have a good working dog, but you should do all initial training in a quiet area, gradually exposing your pup to distractions after he has learned to respond properly to a given behavior.

If your dog scoots away from the noise, fearful of the sudden distraction, but eventually returns to you and resumes targeting work, you should do all training in a quiet area. When he has fully accomplished basic obedience, gradually increase his exposure to distractions, beginning with minor ones first, such as his toys.

A dog that goes after a distraction and forgets what he was targeting will be far more difficult to work with.

You will most definitely want to work one-on-one with a professional trainer. Your pup is independent and possibly dominant and therefore, more difficult to train, especially when distracted.

There are a few general rules you'll need to consider before doing any training, including targeting, which is the start of training. First of all, make sure your puppy is well rested. A tired pup has no stamina and will not be able to work very long. Second, make sure your puppy is not full. It's not a good idea to train him after he eats. In fact, just before mealtime is a terrific time to train. He is hungry and eager to earn his dinner. Third, make sure you begin all puppy kindergarten training in a fenced-in, quiet area. This will ensure the safety and security of your pup, as well as ensure that you will have his complete attention.

There are tests that you can conduct to help evaluate your puppy's distraction threshold. Hopefully, he is capable of ignoring distractions, which will make training him much easier and more enjoyable.

Training Approach

After your puppy has successfully passed the three tests in Chapter 1, he should be ready to begin puppy kindergarten. However, don't start yet. First, you need to learn how to speak "canine." Canine communication uses different ways of conveying messages than what we are used to. In order to teach your puppy properly, you must communicate with him using his own language. Junior will soon learn the meaning of your words through your use of specific cues.

Dogs communicate with all their senses. They convey complex messages through their body language, vocal tones, and scent glands. They show affection through touch and reward through taste. In order for us to communicate with our puppy, we must utilize a similar communication approach. We will concentrate on using vocal tones and visual cues because these are the easiest senses for us to control.

There are three distinct sounds that you must use while training: a high, happy, and enthusiastic tone with praise; a demanding tone with a command; and a low, growly tone with a reprimand. The actual words that you use don't matter, provided you use the same ones for the same circumstances. Be sure to keep the words simple and easy to remember, such as "Good" with the praise tone and "No" with the reprimand tone.

When giving a command, precede the command with

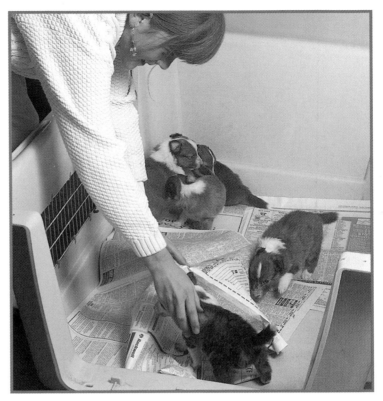

Before you begin training your puppy, you must understand how canines communicate and process information.

your dog's name, such as "Junior, Sit." Say the command only one time and then make sure you back it up. This means that if your puppy doesn't listen, you must quickly place him in the position you requested. For example, you tell him to sit, but he remains standing, looking at you questioningly. You will need to place his little bottom down gently and praise him. This teaches him the meaning of sit.

Never repeat a command. This only teaches your puppy that you weren't serious when you told him the first time. The more you give a command, the less your pup will listen to you. Your voice

Basic training provides your puppy with the confidence and understanding necessary for becoming an obedient, well-adjusted adult.

14

Dogs communicate with one another through body language, vocal tones, and scent glands. Using vocal tones and visual cues, you can effectively communicate with your puppy.

will become background noise, like a radio or television. The noise is there but has no meaning. Say the command once, then back it up.

One way of ensuring that your puppy learns the command without your having to repeat it is to teach him the behavior without any command first. Through targeting, lure him into place with the treat. Do this three to five times and then add the command with the action. After several repetitions, your puppy will begin to associate the command with his action.

There are two distinct body signals that you should use while training. The first is to remain upright when giving a command or reprimand. The second is to crouch down to puppy level when praising, playing, or coaxing. In the beginning of your training sessions, there will be a lot of coaxing when you give a command, so don't become confused with having to crouch down when asking your pup to come and sit with later training procedures as your pup gets older. Puppies require a less dominant approach and will respond better to a more

This American Pit Bull pup takes a moment to relax and enjoy the sun.

Help put your puppy into the correct position if he is confused or having difficulty understanding the command. After doing so, praise him so that he knows what the correct behavior is.

attractive goal. For example, your pup will be more likely to come to you when you are crouched down than if you are standing upright. You look more inviting when crouched and more intimidating when standing upright.

Eye contact is also very important, especially when it comes to reprimanding. Your puppy is more likely to listen to you if you establish eye contact with him. Blinking and looking away from him while you say, "No" will be totally ineffective. You must do the "alpha stare," which means looking him in the eye and maintaining contact until your pup looks away first. Always keep your eyes on him while training.

You need to work with your pup several times a day. Puppies have very short attention spans but love the stimulation, provided you offer it in short, frequent amounts. Keep your training sessions at a length of ten minutes. You never want to force your puppy to work when his attention span is lost. Short training sessions keep your pup looking forward to the next one.

If you are using a food bait, have it fully prepared before you begin the training session, which means already sliced into small morsels and placed in an easy-to-access area, like a pocket or pouch. Junior will not stand around and wait for you to find the treat and break it apart. His mind will wander, and before you know it, he will no longer be paying attention to you. The odors in the grass will be far more interesting.

It would also be a good idea not to be smoking, eating, or drinking while working with your puppy. In order for your puppy to give you his full attention, you need to do the same for him. If you must do any of the other activities, do so when your puppy is released from the work.

PUPPY SOCIALIZATION

The canine is a very social species. They prefer to spend most of their time in each other's company. As a new member of your family pack, your pup will always want to be with you. It is a good idea to let your puppy meet as many people as possible during the formative age between two to six months. The more people

When giving your puppy a command, be sure not to repeat it, or he will think you weren't serious the first time. This trio of Great Dane pups knows how to smile on command.

Puppy Kindergarten

Remain in an upright position when giving your puppy a command or reprimand.

your puppy meets, the better behaved he'll be in the future.

Just as it is important for him to meet new people, it is equally important for him to meet other dogs. Puppies learn many socialization skills from other canines that people cannot effectively teach, which is why it is important to expose Junior to many different canine personalities. A few words of caution on this, however. Puppies are very susceptible to contagious diseases and should not be exposed to strange dogs until they have received all their necessary inoculations. If you already have another dog that is healthy, allow them to play and sleep together. Don't worry about the pup being too small or too boisterous

Your puppy will be more likely to listen to you if you give him the "alpha stare," which means looking him right in the eye. Be sure to maintain eye contact until your puppy looks away first.

Keep training sessions with your puppy short and interesting, which will keep him looking forward to the next one.

for the older dog. Most dogs will ignore many puppy transgressions and will not show aggression unless the puppy is extremely obnoxious. If there is a tousle, it normally consists only of a snarl and/or snap. This is a powerful lesson for the puppy because it teaches him proper behavior.

Once Junior has had all his inoculations, you can take him to meet the neighborhood dogs and join a puppy socialization class. These classes are often offered by kennel clubs, dog day care centers, and some recreation departments. This is similar to placing young children in nursery school so that they can learn social skills and personal interac-

tions. Taking your puppy to socialize with other puppies is a very important part of his behavior training.

Puppy socialization classes normally last less than an hour and meet about four times. The instructor will speak with you regarding behavior problem prevention and basic puppy kindergarten training, and will allow plenty of time for the puppies to play with each other. Junior is guaranteed to go home and sleep for hours.

CHOOSING A TRAINER

There are three distinct approaches to dog training—group, private, and boarding. Each type has positive results when utilized appropriately. Training a puppy

involves several carefully mapped stages. You should not automatically take your puppy to a group training class if he has no idea how to behave. The only group situation that Junior should enter is the puppy socialization class, which allows him to spend most of his time playing with other pups. Prior to a regular group training class, you should meet with a private trainer who will either come to your home or provide a quiet area for puppy training.

There are several reasons why you should begin one-on-one training. First of all, your puppy should not be exposed to other dogs until he has had all of his inoculations. Second, you want to

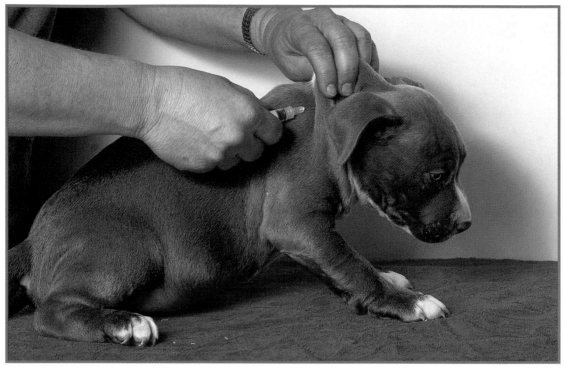

Make sure that your puppy has received all of his inoculations before you let him play with other dogs.

Expose your puppy to as many different canine personalities as possible. This will help him learn important socialization skills that humans can't teach him.

Puppy socialization classes are a good way for your puppy to learn how to interact with other dogs. Classes usually last less than an hour.

ensure that he has a positive training experience, which can only be accomplished by working in a quiet and familiar environment.

You cannot take Junior into a group situation until he is approximately four months old, but you should not wait to train him until that age. He needs to begin learning as young as two months of age. When working with a private trainer, Junior will learn all the basic skills through puppy kindergarten training. Once Junior reaches four months of age, you and he will be ready for the distractions of a group situation.

The one type of training that you should not do is send Junior away to a board-and-train situation, because you and your puppy

need this time to bond. There is no better way to bond than through training and spending time together. Also, learning together is the only way you will be able to communicate effectively with him.

A dog that begins his training at a young age should never need the intense training of the board-and-train situation, which is more useful for an out-of-control adult dog that has owners who are unable to be effective. Through this type of training, the dog will learn his commands. His owners are then taught how to give the commands before their dog is sent home. However, this does not work like magic, because the dog's owners must still be consistent and work with their dog

in order to maintain the training. Otherwise, all the trainer's work is useless.

To sum up your protocol, do the following: Begin puppy kindergarten with a professional private trainer. Once that training is mostly complete, your puppy should be finished with his immunity-building inoculations and ready to socialize. At this time, take your puppy to the socialization classes, but continue to complete the puppy kindergarten with the private trainer. Once the puppy kindergarten is complete and your puppy has gone through a set of puppy socialization classes, you can sign him up for group training sessions as a means of distraction-proofing him.

Choosing a good trainer is very important to the well-

The personal attention that a puppy receives from one-on-one training enables him to feel comfortable, relaxed, and focused.

At four months of age, a puppy is able to deal with the distractions of a group training situation, provided that he has already learned his basic skills.

Training can be a wonderful bonding experience for you and your new puppy. These two friends share a learning moment.

being of your puppy. Be sure to ask your veterinarian for a referral. Most veterinarians are very conscientious about suggesting someone with a good reputation and professional attitude. Another source is to contact the National Association of Dog Obedience Instructors at 2286 E. Steel Rd., St. Johns, MI 48879. The American Society for the Prevention of Cruelty to Animals and the Humane Society of the United States might also be helpful. Your local kennel club or breeder may recommend someone.

When you contact a trainer, be certain to ask about his or her experience and training methods, and ask to observe a training session. The trainer should be knowledgeable about your puppy's breed. If you have

Choosing the perfect trainer for your puppy can be a difficult job. Your veterinarian should be able to suggest someone with a good reputation and professional attitude.

any current problems such as housetraining, chewing, or mouthing, mention these concerns. Will that trainer be able to help you solve these problems? Make sure that the trainer is flexible enough to meet your scheduling needs. The last thing you need is to begin the training and then cancel due to time conflicts.

Through your telephone conversation, you should be able to determine whether or not you and the trainer are compatible. The trainer should make you feel relaxed and confident. You do not want to begin the puppy training with someone who is pushy, domineering, or lacking the answers to your many questions. You must be comfortable with

and confident in that person, because you are placing the well-being of your beloved "child" in their hands. The dog trainer must be a combination of a psychologist, biologist, nutritionist, and assertiveness counselor. It is only with knowledge in all these categories that you will receive positive results.

The trainer you choose should be knowledgeable about your breed, as well as help make you feel comfortable, relaxed, and confident.

Basic Commands

Everything you do with your puppy must be approached in a positive manner. Training is no different. If you want your pup to do what you ask and look forward to working with you, he must have fun while he is performing. That is where puppy kindergarten comes in.

Puppy kindergarten is a form of play training, which is the best way to obtain fast results that last a lifetime. Your puppy thinks he is playing when in actuality he is learning. A puppy that is having fun will maintain a longer attention span and look forward to each training session.

Begin each training session by having Junior target, which obtains his attention and prepares him for learning new behaviors. In fact, he'll easily learn how to sit within the first couple minutes of the targeting exercise.

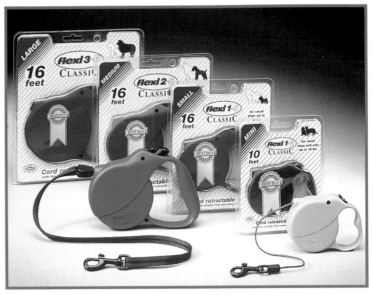

Retractable leashes provide dogs freedom while allowing the owner to keep command at all times. Leashes are available in a wide variety of lengths for all breeds of dog. Photo courtesy of Flexi-USA, Inc.

TARGET AND SIT

Begin the first training session by giving Junior a treat and saying, "Good" as he takes it from you. Do this several times. Next, hold the treat in your fingers, place your hand with-in his reach, and wait for him to touch your hand with his nose. Say, "Good, dog!" and give him the treat. Repeat this two or three times. Next, move your hand a little to the left and then to the right. As Junior keeps his nose on the target, praise him and give him his treat. Add an up-and-down motion. Each time Junior follows the target, reward him.

Now we'll teach Junior to sit. Place your targeting hand in front of your pup's nose and lift it slightly upward toward his eyes. As you do this, say, "Junior, Sit." Your pup will be watching his target and as his head moves upward, his rear end will go down, like a see-saw. The moment Junior's rear end touches the ground, praise him and give him his reward.

Targeting should be one of the first commands you teach your puppy. Be sure to praise him each time he keeps his nose on the target.

As you teach your puppy how to come to you on command, gradually increase your steps backward. This way, he learns to come to you from increasingly longer distances.

To teach the come and sit exercise, make sure that your puppy either has a leash on or is securely fenced-in.

Through this exercise, you are teaching Junior to stop whatever he is doing, remain still, and pay attention. This is very important because your puppy can't learn if you do not have his attention first. Junior will learn the target and sit exercise within a few minutes. Yes, puppies do learn that fast.

COME AND SIT

One of the most important things your puppy will learn is the come command. Due to Junior's age, this is one of the easiest commands to teach. Your puppy is very insecure and will be until he reaches the age of five months. He'll want to be near you at all times.

Teach your puppy to sit for things that he wants, such as food or a special treat.

Puppy Kindergarten

Put your targeting hand under your pup's nose. Make sure your puppy is on his leash or in a secure fenced-in area for this exercise. Let Junior smell the treats and then step backward two or three steps as you say, "Junior, come," in a happy tone of voice. He'll immediately follow his target. Praise him enthusiastically as he comes toward you.

When you stop, bring your hand over his head to an area just between his eyes so that he must look upward. Be sure your hand is not more than two inches from his nose, or he'll likely jump up. While he's looking up, say, "Junior, sit." As soon as his rear end goes down, praise him and give him his treat.

Continually increase your steps backward as you practice the come command. This way, Junior will learn to come to you from increasingly longer distances. Always make him sit when he arrives. The last thing you want Junior to learn is to come and then leave or to come and jump up. A come and sit ensures that his attention stays on you and teaches him appropriate behavior patterns.

When Junior learns how to come and sit with no difficulty, attach a lightweight leash (anywhere from four to six feet in length) to his regular neck collar. Let him drag the leash while you work with him. This will allow Junior to get used to the feel of the leash without having it pulled on or used in a manner that he does not understand.

Round Robin

When Junior is able to come and sit, it's time to involve the entire family. First of all, everyone must do the come and sit exercises with him individually, so that he learns to listen to everyone. Then, two family members should stand about six feet apart, facing each other. These are the positions for the round robin game, which is a fundamental means of teaching your puppy how to perform specific behaviors such as sit,

Puppies need to be constantly rewarded for a job well done. Used accordingly, treats play a major part in helping your puppy learn his basic commands.

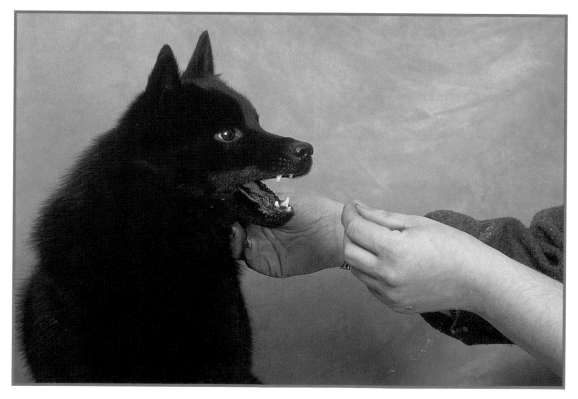

The sit command is one of the most important commands that your puppy will learn. It means that he must stop whatever he is doing and pay attention.

stay, down, and come.

This type of training has many benefits. Your puppy is able to maintain a longer attention span because he is enjoying himself. He learns how to work for everyone in the family, not just one person. Also, the physical activity will make him tired. A tired puppy stays out of trouble, giving you peace of mind for a while.

Begin by calling Junior to come to you. As soon as he sits and receives his treat, the next person calls him. Junior will come to each member of the family and sit facing you. Go back and forth a few times, then increase the distance between you by taking one big step backward while the other person has Junior's attention. You can continue increasing the distance up to

about 30 feet. More than that would be too much on Junior's little puppy legs.

If Junior becomes distracted during his travels between family members, the person who last called him should try to regain his attention by putting a treat under Junior's nose. If this is not enough, then that person should take hold of the leash and bring Junior to him. This is very important, because Junior will quickly figure out whose voice has meaning and whose does not. Dogs will not listen to people who do not back up their commands.

HEEL AND SIT

The round robin game and the come and sit exercises can easily be transferred into the heel and sit work, because Junior

already knows how to target. All you have to do is transfer your target to your left side instead of holding it in front of you. Junior will then go to your left side and sit.

Begin by having Junior do a come and sit. As soon as he sits, place yourself at his right side, your leg even with his shoulder. This is the proper heeling position. It is important that Junior learns to remain in this position, otherwise he will not be attentive.

Once at Junior's side, maintain his attention by keeping your target on your left leg at knee level. When his nose targets on your hand, offer the reward as you praise him. When he's finished with his treat say, "Junior, heel," and take a step forward on your left leg. Moving your left leg first

A tired puppy is one of the benefits of training. This adorable puppy takes time out to take a nap in his favorite tree.

Before you progress in your training, make sure that your puppy knows the previous lesson.

Puppies have a natural tendency to follow their nose and wander off. Learning the basic commands could help keep him out of danger.

becomes Junior's visual cue for the heel command. He'll learn to move forward as your leg moves forward.

Go only one step and stop. Junior will most likely follow his target and move forward with you. As soon as he does, praise him. When you stop, say, "Junior, sit." As soon as he sits, give him the treat. Keep increasing your steps each time you do the heel exercise. Within a short time, you and Junior will be walking 5, 10, 20 steps and more. Once you get this far, you can begin incorporating turns. Do a turn and stop directly after the turn. This will keep Junior at your side. During later training, executing turns will be the best means of maintaining Junior's attention.

If your puppy seems disinterested in his target, replace it with something more inviting. Remember that the reward does not always have to be food.

The down command can be difficult for puppies to learn because they have to assume a submissive position. It's good to teach this command early in their development before they begin to test their position in the family "pack."

If, at any time, Junior becomes disenchanted by his target and more interested in the last stick he passed, place the reward under his nose and draw him closer to you. Decrease the amount of steps between your start and stop. Perhaps his current reward is not inviting enough. Try something else. If he were interested in that stick, maybe holding it would maintain his attention. The reward does not always have to be food.

Another thing you can do to maintain his interest once he can heel successfully is to change your pace now and then. Junior must learn to remain at your side whether you are walking slow or fast. In fact, one of the ways to obtain the attention of a distracted pup is to jog a bit. Most pups will eagerly run after a fast-moving playmate. Just don't let him think you're a playmate, because

Always have your puppy arrive and sit before awaiting his next command. This Rottweiler demonstrates model behavior for his friends.

Because little puppies are always in motion, teaching the stay command could be a challenge. Try to be patient and stay firm and consistent in your role as leader.

Junior must always know that you're the boss. Do any pace changes in short bursts. Always praise Junior as he catches up with you. If he overshoots, turn to the right and lure him back to your side.

DOWN

The next command on your training agenda is the down, which is initially taught during the round robin game. It should be interspersed with the sit command. For example, Junior sits on one round and sits and lies down before the next person calls him on the next round.

The down can be difficult to teach because it is a submissive position. If Junior has a dominant personality, he will not learn the down command easily. However, this is even more reason to teach him this command as early as you can. While your puppy is young, he is less apt to test his pack position than when he reaches the more independent age of 18 to 20 weeks.

Targeting is the easiest means of teaching Junior to lie down on his own. Place the treat between your thumb and middle finger. When Junior arrives and sits, let him smell the treat as you point down at the ground between his front toes. His head will dip downward. Most puppies will follow their heads and bring the rest of their bodies down as well. If your puppy does not do so on his own, gently apply pressure on his shoulder blades. He should easily drop onto his belly. As soon as he has completed the

criterion for this command, i.e., is lying down, give him lots of praise and his treat.

Be absolutely certain to vary your request for the down. This is very important, because you don't want Junior to believe that he should arrive and lie down. He should always come in and sit first, then await his next command. Dogs are easily pattern trained. If you repeat something as few as three times, Junior will learn the pattern and anticipate your commands. While it's nice to know that Junior really wants to please you

that much, it does not mean that he's completely obedience trained.

STAY

The next command Junior will learn is the stay, which is often the most difficult. Young dogs are constantly in motion and remaining in the same spot is not on the top of their agenda. The stay command will need to be taught through a gradual increase of your criterion using successive approximation.

Successive approximation is used whenever gradually increasing the criterion for any given exercise. For

Most puppies are eager to please their owners and will try very hard to obey their commands. Make sure that praise and a reward are ready for your puppy when he completes a job.

example, when you taught Junior to heel by taking one step and built on that, you used successive approximation. As he accomplished a couple steps, you went on to more steps in between each stop and sit. Before long, you were walking ten steps and doing turns. You successively increased the criterion for each ultimate reward—the treat.

Begin teaching this exercise by first playing the round robin game. When Junior arrives and sits, place the palm of your hand in front of his nose and say, "Junior, Stay." Hold the treat near his nose, but don't give it to him for three to five sec-

onds. Praise him as he remains in place. Give him his treat, and the next person should call him to come. Each time you have him come and sit, increase the amount of time that Junior has to maintain a stay before receiving his reward.

Because you'll have a lot to do within a short time frame, looking at your watch is not something you can coordinate. You can more easily count the seconds by using, "Good, boys." One second equals one "Good, boy." The first time you do a stay, you'll say, "Good, boy," one to two times. The next time, Junior gets 2 to 3 "Good, boys," and so on,

until he can remain in place at least 30 seconds.

By the time your reach five or six words of praise, Junior may start popping up and trying to go to the next person, who might be more willing to offer a treat for a simple sit. You can prevent this by stepping on his leash when he arrives and sits before you. If he gets up, you can easily bring him back into position and repeat your stay command. After replacing him in approximately the same location again, tell him to stay, only this time, shorten the amount of time to two or three "Good, boys." Sometimes you need to regress in order to progress.

Make training sessions fun and interesting for your puppy so that he looks forward to learning. These two friends might be having more fun than they actually are working.

36

The main goal of your training is to have your puppy willingly stay in one position for a length of time. This Great Dane has no problems as long as he has his toys nearby.

When working with a puppy, everything needs to remain as positive as possible. Going back to a comfortable zone (in this case, less time in the stay) increases Junior's desire to please you.

Each time you have a training session, increase your pup's stay time. In a few weeks, he'll be able to remain in one spot without any problem. Practice the stay exercise with the down position. Remember to vary all the exercises in order to keep Junior attentive.

When Junior is able to remain in the sit/stay for more than 30 seconds, it is time to introduce the next variable—moving around him as he remains sitting. This needs to be done with a gradual increase of movement. You begin by stepping side to side while you face Junior. The next time you do a stay command, you step on either side of him from head to back legs on both sides. When Junior can remain sitting throughout your movements, you can begin walking in circles around him.

If your puppy gets up, put him back into position as close to the original location where you told him to perform his sit/stay. This way, he learns to remain where you told him to stay, not where he chooses to stay.

As Junior accepts your walking around him, try doing so in both directions. Then, begin to increase your distance as you move around him. Add a foot or two of space between you and Junior each time he does a sit/stay. Within several training sessions, you should be able to get six feet away from him as he remains in his sit/stay.

Practice this exercise with the down/stay as well. The only difference is that instead of stepping in front of Junior, you'll begin your side-to-side movements along his right side and proceed to walk around him by going around his back end first. This way, Junior is less likely to get up.

Your puppy should be able to remain calmly in his position while you walk around him. This Airedale Terrier can't resist the chance to play.

Housetraining and Behavior Modification

The first thing on any new puppy owner's mind is the amount of time it will take to housetrain Junior. Either through past experiences or hearing the nightmares of other puppy owners, you might believe this process can take upward of six months—not so. A puppy as young as eight weeks can learn the appropriate relief area within one week. However, this does not mean you can trust him to run loose in the house. It only means that Junior will learn that when he is taken to that area, he goes potty. When he is indoors, he must still be confined and watched until he reaches about four months.

CRATE TRAINING AND HOUSETRAINING

There are several ways to ensure housetraining success: containment, setting a schedule, praising Junior when he does the right thing, constantly watching the puppy's behavior, and tricks to make things more fun.

Having a place to contain Junior will make the entire process much easier. You will need a crate or pen of an area not much larger than your puppy. If you wish to get a crate that Junior will fit in when he is full grown, use cinder blocks or a crate divider to make the crate temporarily smaller.

Whenever you cannot spend time with Junior, he should be in the crate.

Most new puppy owners are concerned about the amount of time that it will take to train their puppy. Most puppies are very eager to please their owner and enjoy spending time with them.

Junior will easily accept crate training because it simulates a den-like atmosphere where a mother dog would prefer to bear and raise her young. In the wild, puppies are taught by their mothers to do their business outside their den. With these instincts already in place, Junior will learn to contain himself while in his crate.

Crate training is very easy and should never be forced. Begin teaching proper crate manners from the first day that Junior comes home. Place his toys, bed, and water in the crate. Feed him in his crate. These things will immediately give Junior positive associations with the crate and he will quickly settle in. Allow him to have access to his crate when he roams freely. He needs a room to call his own, just in case he gets tired or nervous in his surroundings.

If you have to leave Junior by himself for long hours at a time, you should not leave him in his crate. This is not humane. It may take longer to housetrain him, but there are ways to make him feel less confined and to facilitate proper potty associations. In this situation, place Junior's crate inside a pen, like an exercise pen or larger chain-link pen. You still don't want to give him a lot of space, but just enough that he can stretch his legs and move around a bit. The surface should be easy to clean, such as linoleum, concrete, or tile. Obtain either a small child's pool or metal tray with low sides. Place it on the side of the pen opposite his crate, water, and bed. Fill the container with dirt, wood chips, or sod. This will simulate the outdoors, and Junior will be most likely to do his business there. Dogs simply prefer to eliminate in an area that will soak it up.

There are some puppies, such as those kept in crates and never let out while being raised, that will potty in their crates. It'll be more difficult to housetrain this type of dog, but it can still be done through proper feeding and scheduling. You may have to take the bed out of the crate for a short period of time, because as long as there's something there to soak up the urine, the pup will continue to wet on it.

Setting a schedule is one of the most important aspects of housetraining because it helps Junior to learn more quickly. You'll need to schedule his relief times to coincide with his feeding, play, and nap times. You can be assured that every puppy will have to go potty within ten minutes after eating (this time elongates as the puppy ages), directly upon waking from a nap, and shortly after playing.

Knowing these times and

Whenever you cannot be around to supervise your puppy, he should be in his crate. Putting his food, toys, and warm bedding inside will help him feel more comfortable.

Your puppy should adapt well to the crate because it simulates a den-like atmosphere. Allow him to have access to his crate at all times.

Putting dirt, wood chips, or sod where your puppy eliminates simulates the outdoors, where he is most likely to do his business. Dogs prefer to eliminate in an area that will soak it up.

12 pm: Feed Junior.
12:15 pm: Take Junior outside to go potty. Continue to take Junior outside every hour or directly after a nap or play period.
4 pm: Feed Junior.
4:15 pm: Take Junior outside.
(Take him outside every hour, especially if you are playing with him. Don't give Junior any food after his 4 pm meal and take up his water around 8 pm.)
11 pm: Take Junior outside for his last potty time of the day and make sure that he eliminates before putting him to bed in his crate. Put an ice cube in his water dish. This will keep him hydrated through the night, plus it's a great treat for your puppy.

Sometimes puppies become so distracted by the outdoors that they forget why they came out. You are standing there waiting and waiting, and all Junior is doing is smelling the daisies. This can become very tiresome. Instead of allowing Junior to become distracted, return him to his crate and try again a half an hour later. The last thing you need is to have to wait outside while Junior wanders around. This can be especially frustrating in bad weather. Junior needs to relieve himself immediately, and then he can be allowed to play and explore.

One of the ways to make housetraining even easier is to teach Junior to go potty on command, which will save you a lot of time waiting for him to do his business. Begin by taking him outside as soon as he wakes up in the morning. He'll most

remaining consistent will make it easier to take Junior to his relief area before an accident occurs. It will also contribute to a more positive relationship between you and your puppy.

Following is a sample schedule to get you started:
6 am: Take Junior outside as soon as you wake up.
6:15 am: Feed Junior.
6:25 am: Take Junior outside.

Take Junior outside every hour after that to go potty. (This will need to be continued until Junior reaches three months of age. At this time, you can begin to elongate the intervals between relief times, gradually working up to four hours by the time Junior is six months of age. Many dogs can hold it for much longer than four hours, but it is not fair to make them do so.)

If you have to leave your puppy alone for an extended length of time, do not leave him in his crate. Placing his crate inside a larger exercise pen or putting up a baby gate would work just fine.

definitely have to go potty. Say a single word over and over, such as Hurry, Potty, Business, etc. As soon as Junior goes, praise him and give him a treat. Every time you take him outside, say the potty word until he performs. Always praise and make a fuss over him when he responds. Puppies become very excited when they begin connecting your words with their actions. Within a few days, Junior will be going potty on command.

Always keep an eye on Junior when he's outside of his crate or pen. He will show telltale signs when he needs to go potty. First, if you have always taken him out the same door to his

Housetraining can be a much easier process if you establish a schedule for eating, feeding, and eliminating.

relief area, he'll most likely head in that direction. Second, if he is not near the door, he'll circle and sniff. Another possible cue is when he sits and stares at you. Many puppies that have a good idea of where they must do

Puppies will usually try to communicate to their people when they have to go potty, either by circling or sniffing at the door or staring at their owner.

their business will stare at their people and try to use telepathic vibrations to get the message across. Obviously, this rarely works,

so if you see any of these behaviors, you need to get him outside quickly or there is sure to be an accident.

If you practice these

aforementioned procedures and still experience accidents, try teaching Junior to tell you when he needs to go outside. Because he can't stand up and say, "I've gotta go now!" we need to communicate in a more universal manner. Teach Junior to ring a bell to let you know.

Hang a large bell on the doorknob of the same door that Junior passes through to go to his relief area. The bell needs to hang low enough for him to reach it and make it move. Before you take him outside each time, rub a little cheese on the bell. Show it to Junior. When he licks the cheese, the bell will move and make noise. As soon as you hear the bell ring, quickly take him outside to his relief area

You should take your puppy outside to eliminate first thing in the morning and right before he goes to sleep at night to avoid any unnecessary accidents.

Although playing around can be fun, inappropriate behavior like jumping up should be immediately corrected.

and give him his potty command. As soon as he relieves himself, give him a treat. Wow! Junior just got double reinforcement for doing the right thing. If you wish to remain outside and play, fine. This will all reinforce how pleasant life is when one maintains control. In a week or less, Junior will be going directly to the door and ringing the bell, and you will have a housetrained dog.

PREVENTING BAD HABITS

An ounce of prevention is worth a pound of cure, or so the old tale goes. This is especially true in the case of raising a puppy. Prevent the problem so that you don't have to cure it later.

Young puppies have not yet established bad habits. The best means of ensuring that Junior doesn't become destructive is not to allow it

in the first place. While you may think, "Oh, he's just a puppy. He'll get over it," this is not the case. Whatever you allow him to do as a pup, he will also do as an adult dog. Yes, a young puppy can't do a lot of damage, but an older dog can. For example, you allow Junior to jump on you when he's little. What happens when he weighs over 50 pounds? You get scratches on your legs, your clothing is ruined, and he knocks down your elderly parents. You are setting precedents in Junior's life from the very beginning. Simply don't allow him to do something while he's young that you don't want him to continue doing later. Junior will not hold a grudge against you, nor will his feelings get hurt. Puppies actually become more relaxed when they

understand their surroundings. Being consistent from the beginning will accomplish these goals.

There are many stages in a puppy's life. Junior will go through teething, testing, and hierarchy discovery all in his first six months. Each of these things presents different challenges.

Teething begins at three months of age and continues until Junior reaches nine months. While Junior may have oral fixations as a 2-month-old pup, it's not until around 12 weeks that his front baby teeth will begin falling out. By 16 weeks, he'll be losing his incisors and by 5 months, he'll be losing his molars. Throughout this period, new teeth will be coming in and causing much discomfort.

Make sure that you keep

Puppy Kindergarten

Junior away from your furniture, carpets, and moldings. Wood objects in particular, like tables and chair legs, will bear the brunt of sore gums. Instead of having to replace everything you own and soon despising your puppy, teach Junior from day one what he can and cannot put his mouth on. This means watching him closely.

You need to provide Junior with a variety of chew toys and keep an eye on him to make sure he chews the appropriate things. A good way to keep Junior's attention on his own toys is to put his kibble inside hollow toys such as Buster Cubes and discs, sterilized bones, and Kong toys. If you feed your pup in this manner for the first three months, it will ensure that he will never touch anything other than his toys. After this period, you can feed him in a dish, and Junior will most likely maintain his fixation on his toys because he has been properly conditioned.

When you cannot watch Junior, he must be put in his crate or contained in an area that is puppy proofed, which will prevent any mishaps while you are away. Junior will feel more relaxed, and you will be able to rest easy knowing that your house will still be in one piece when you return.

If you see Junior testing out a chair leg to see if it's as tasty as his chew toy, push him away as you growl at him. Immediately return his attention to his toy by playing with him. This will redirect him from the

When puppies begin teething, which is usually around three months of age, they have a tendency to chew on anything that looks appetizing. Provide your puppy with safe chew toys, like a bone or plastic ball.

Puppies will chew on anything while they are teething. If you can't supervise him, make sure that he is contained in a safe area and given appropriate toys.

46

Be careful to get your message across as clearly as possible when you are communicating with your puppy.

misbehavior to something positive, which is how all puppy training should be.

There are several ways you can make teething a little easier for Junior. One is to offer him ice cubes. If Junior does not like plain ice cubes, freeze some chicken bouillon in an ice cube tray and make puppy popsicles. Another teething treat is a frozen, wet washcloth. Allow Junior to gnaw on the washcloth until it melts. The ideal teething treat is a frozen marrow bone, which can be purchased at your local grocery store. They are sold as soup bones filled with bits of meat and marrow. Not only will Junior enjoy the frozen bone, but it can be used over and over again by adding peanut butter or cheese and freezing

it for use as a future reward.

Testing and hierarchical discovery go hand in hand. Puppies are born with the ability to train their people. We, on the other hand, have to learn to speak canine in order to train our puppy properly. This means communicating on a very basic principle—the all-or-none law. Junior can either always do something or never do something.

Dogs don't understand gray areas such as, "It's okay this time, but not next time." For example, Junior jumps on you. You allow it because you're wearing jeans at the time, but what happens when you're dressed for work or for an evening out? Junior doesn't know the difference between nice and casual clothes. He

only knows that if he jumps on you, he gets attention. He learned this concept very quickly when he jumped on you the first time and you petted him. To keep Junior from jumping on you when you wear nice clothes, you'll need to teach him not to jump on you at all.

"Oh, he's only a puppy," you say. Yes, but he will grow up knowing how to manipulate you. Never give Junior any attention when he misbehaves, including placating him when he shows fear or aggression. This serves to reinforce the bad behavior. When Junior barks at someone, the last thing you should do is crouch down and cuddle with him saying, "It's okay honey. You'll be all right." You just reinforced the behavior!

47

Stop bad behavior before it starts. Make your puppy earn your praise by sitting and looking up at you for attention and petting.

Make Junior earn your attention and praise by doing something good, such as sitting and looking up at you for attention instead of jumping. Give him his food only after he sits, not while he's jumping around. Don't let him out the door until he sits first. Don't pet him unless he performs a command for you. This puts you in the "top dog" position. Teaching Junior to do as you request before he receives anything maintains your dominance without having to be harsh in any way.

These concepts should be applied to every situation, such as raiding the garbage can, jumping on furniture and counters, chewing shoes and towels, digging in the yard, and excessive barking. Saying, "Stop it, stop it," in a placating tone of voice will not cure the problem. You must take charge and nip it in the bud. As soon as Junior shows any signs of doing something wrong, such as sniffing at the garbage, digging, or putting a paw on the furniture, correct him immediately by pushing him away as you growl and redirect his attention onto a toy.

CURING BAD HABITS

If Junior has already wrapped you around his paw and begun misbehaving, you need to cure the problems in a way that he will understand. Dogs never hit each other, yell, swear, or hold grudges. Thus, if you use these behaviors to try to cure your pup of bad habits, Junior will not understand. Instead, you'll be causing worse problems, like fear biting and submissive urination. Use canine language to make your point. Junior will understand and learn faster, with less confusion.

Jumping

Jumping is one of the most common bad habits. Initially, Junior is jumping up to say hello. When dogs greet each other, they first touch noses. As he learns that jumping up earns him attention, he begins jumping up as a means of demanding your attention. Unless you don't care about going to work or out for the evening with paw prints on your clothing, you should teach Junior that jumping up is not what good puppies do.

The easiest means of teaching this is to first

Dogs don't understand yelling, hitting, or holding grudges. Correcting your puppy in ways that he will understand will help him learn much faster and with less confusion.

Learning basic commands, such as down, will help curb problem behaviors.

ignore him when he jumps on you. You can move back as he's about to put his paws on you. Without you to land on, Junior discovers that jumping up has no benefits, and he will stop the behavior. You do have to be timely, because if Junior does get his paws on you, the correction won't work.

Another means of curing jumping is to make a "no-jump" box, which has many uses. A "no-jump" box is a small metal can, like a bandage box, tea tin, or coffee can. Place 15 pennies inside and close the lid securely. You may want to make several no-jump boxes and place them strategically near doors, in the kitchen, and in the family room. This way you're always prepared.

When Junior jumps up, shake the can firmly in an up-and-down motion, once or twice. You won't need to do it more than this,

because the noise burst will make Junior move away. As soon as all four feet are on the ground, make him sit and then praise him. Once he's sitting, pat his head and praise him. This teaches Junior that good things come to puppies that sit for attention.

Chewing on You

Puppies are very orally oriented. They will put their mouths on anything, especially you. This may be cute while Junior has his little baby teeth, but it will not be cute as his jaw pressure increases. This behavior should be stopped immediately.

As soon as Junior puts his mouth on you, take him by the scruff of the neck, look him in his eyes, and growl. Continue to hold him and stare at him until he looks away first. This is very important, because if you look away first, you are

giving in to him, regardless of the fact that you are holding him by his scruff. Never look away first. Also, be aware that Junior's blinking is the first indication of his submission. You can release Junior after a blink or two. Holding him longer would be counterproductive.

Please note that this correction must be done quickly and firmly or it can backfire on you. If you do this incorrectly, Junior will become more tenacious and start biting on purpose. If you are not comfortable with this procedure, try spraying something bitter on your hands just before playing with Junior. He'll hate the taste and immediately let go of your hand. Puppies remember whether something tasted good or bad. Why put their mouths on something really yucky when other things, like food-filled toys, are available?

Chewing on Household Items

Chewing on household items is a common occurrence as puppies explore their surroundings. At first, they don't put their mouths on things to chew them, but to see if something is edible. As puppies develop and begin to teethe, their purpose changes. They begin chewing as a form of relief for their sore gums. Unless you want to lose everything you own, including your puppy, start teaching Junior which things he can and cannot chew on. Namely, he can chew on his own toys, but not on anything that is yours.

There are several ways

Puppies love to chew—on anything! However, don't let this become an uncontrollable problem that you can't fix later.

you can correct Junior, and keep in mind that there will be little need for corrections provided you are always with him when he is outside his enclosure. One way is to use your no-jump box to distract him from chewing the inappropriate object. Then replace his attention onto his own toy by making noise with it. Growl at Junior as you firmly shake the can up and down, once or twice. Present a toy and praise Junior as soon as he puts his mouth on his own toy.

Another means of correcting this problem is to do the same procedure as when Junior tried chewing on you. Take him by the scruff of the neck, look him in the eyes, and growl. When he shows submission, let go and turn his attention onto one of his toys by making noise with it. A squeaky stuffed toy would

definitely grab his attention. A Choo Hoof, or Nylabone®, would work well, too. Remember that you must be quick and firm with this correction for it to work.

When dogs show displeasure, their reaction is always quick and firm. As soon as the other dog

submits, the correction is over and both dogs are friends again. This is the same approach you should take when training your puppy. Never hold a grudge or show malice. Always direct, watch, and communicate in a way that Junior understands.

A well-behaved dog is a happy dog. Although it may take time and patience, training your puppy to become an obedient adult dog is well worth the effort.

Fun Activities for You and Your Puppy

Although Junior may be too young and inexperienced to begin going to dog shows, you can teach him tricks while he is working on his basic training. In fact, taking a break now and then from the routine and teaching a trick can make a training session more exciting. Teaching Junior how to shake paws is a great place to begin. However, if your puppy tends to put his paw on you to show dominance or for attention, you must use the canine "all-or-none" law, which means keeping his paws off of you until he learns that dominant behavior is not acceptable.

Junior must be reliable in a sit/stay before you can begin, however. Many dogs become very excited when performing tricks and need to be able to remain in control long enough to listen while distracted.

SHAKING HANDS
1. Place Junior in a sit/stay and face him.
2. Hold the treat in one hand (this will be your target hand) and hold your other hand, palm up, near the paw you want to shake.
3. Using your target hand, bring Junior's head to the side as you say, "Junior, Shake." As his head follows the target, his weight will also go in that direction, taking it off of the leg you wish to lift and shake.

4. Tap the lifting leg with the fingers of your outstretched hand. When Junior moves that leg, praise him and give him the treat.

This exercise, as with all exercises, will use successive approximation. Each time you have Junior do this trick, you will require that he completes more of the criterion for the final result before he receives his praise and reward.

The first time you ask for the shake, all you'll require is for the leg to move. The second time, you'll require the leg to lift slightly. Each successive request to shake will require Junior to lift his leg higher. As he learns to lift his leg, he will also acquire

Shaking hands is one of the many fun tricks that you can teach your puppy. This furry Keeshond is a natural.

Puppies are a great source of fun and are usually willing to do most anything, provided that you are there with them.

Be sure not to push your puppy too hard in his training or he will begin to lose interest.

After your puppy can successfully shake your hand, you can teach him how to wave.

two targets. The first will be his nose following your hand. The second will be his foot aiming for the upturned palm of your other hand.

At first, target number two is held very close to the ground, so that Junior doesn't have to lift his leg high to accomplish the minor goal. He'll quickly discover that the behavior you are looking for is for his foot to touch your hand. The first time he does so, give him lots of praise and a treat. Each time, hold your hand a little higher, so Junior must lift his leg higher to achieve the second target.

Most puppies accomplish this trick within a few training sessions. Because you make it possible to achieve this goal quickly through your use of shifting his body position and building on small goals until reaching the full picture, Junior will not become confused.

Once Junior is doing his shake for a few weeks, you can start to ask for a "right" or "left" shake. All you need to do is begin pairing the words right or left with your current shake, then switch the signals, gradually building on the criterion for the other side. Be sure to switch your target hands accordingly.

WAVING

The next behavior you can teach is the wave. Junior already has the building blocks for this exercise, because he can lift his paw on command. Transferring the shake into a wave will require that you first teach Junior to shake with your target hands at a distance, instead of within easy reach of his lifted paw.

Begin by sitting a foot or two away when you ask for the shake. Now he'll have to reach his paw forward in order to touch your target hand. Be sure to praise and reward him for each minor increment. When Junior is stretching his paw forward reliably, tell him, "Junior, wave," as you offer your target hand, just out of his reach. He may not understand the verbal command at this time, but will identify with the visual signal. He'll see your outstretched hand and know that he is to put his paw in it. When he reaches forward, you'll allow his paw to rest in your open palm, but will move it up and down twice as you praise him, "Good, Junior. Good wave."

Do this a couple times, teaching Junior that "wave" means his paw will be moved in an up-and-down motion. During the next training session when you ask for the wave, don't let Junior's paw touch your open palm. Keep your hand just out of his reach and move it up and down. Junior will try to put his paw in your hand and will also be moving it up and down. As he does so, praise him and give him his treat. He just accomplished the wave trick.

Slowly build on the amount of times he waves by making him move his paw once more for each wave request before receiving his treat. Don't ask for more than three or four up-and-down paw movements.

SITTING UP

Another trick that can be taught from the base of a sit/stay is to sit up on the haunches. This is commonly called "The Beg," but for the purposes of this book, it will be called the "Sit Up," because begging is actually a behavior problem and not one to be promoted.

Begin by putting Junior in a sit/stay with his rear end placed in a corner of a wall or kitchen cabinets. This type of backdrop will allow him to lean up and back without risking a chance of falling over backward.

1. Hold your target hand with the treat between your thumb and middle finger over Junior's head, point your index finger skyward, and say, "Junior, up." The target hand must not be more than

Although learning tricks takes a lot of practice, puppies don't mind working hard if it involves a fun treat.

Puppy Kindergarten

a few inches over Junior's nose, or he'll feel the need to leap upward to reach it. Hold it almost within his reach but not close enough for him to take the treat from you.

2. As Junior strains to take the treat, he'll put all his weight on his haunches. As soon as he does so, praise before he receives his bridge and reward.

You may need to offer a helping paw. Young dogs have a difficult time with balance because their skeletal and muscular systems are not yet fully developed. Allow Junior to rest a paw on your arm or

You may need to give your puppy a little extra help while he is learning his new tricks. Here, this pup gets a helping hand in "sitting up."

him and give him the reward.

3. The next time you ask him to sit up, don't give him his reward until you see his forelegs leave the ground at least an inch.

Each time you practice sitting up, make sure you require Junior's front feet to leave the ground just a little more each time

hand as his body rises upward to reach his target. This will ensure that he doesn't fall and hurt himself or stop trying due to frustration.

All trick training must be loads of fun for the puppy. If it becomes frustrating, you will lose your puppy's attention. If this happens,

rethink your procedures. Maybe you were asking for too much at one time. Go back to a smaller goal and gradually build on that. All training is a matter of attaining smaller goals before reaching the ultimate goal. Take your time and be very patient. Every puppy is different and learns at a different rate.

The next round of tricks can't be taught until Junior knows how to do a down/stay. These tricks include the tummy up, roll over, and crawl. Each, in turn, builds upon the former.

TUMMY UP

The tummy up involves teaching Junior to roll onto his back and remain there until you say the trick is completed. The signal for completion is your praise.

1. Begin with Junior in a down/stay.

2. Show him your target hand, complete with treat inside. Allow him to touch your hand with his nose.

3. Draw his head toward his shoulders as you say, "Junior, tummy up." When his nose reaches back toward his shoulder, praise and give him his treat.

4. The next time, he doesn't get his reward until his nose actually touches his shoulder.

You will see his entire body start to shift at this point. It has to in order for him to reach around to target properly on your hand. Be sure to praise him as soon as you see the shift.

5. Keep requesting more and more movement for each successive tummy up command.

Your puppy can learn how to "sit up" from the base of a sit/stay position.

Teach your puppy to roll onto his back for a relaxing and soothing tummy rub.

When Junior reaches the point when he is lying on his back, tummy up, praise him and give him the treat, then tell him to stay, using the same visual and verbal cues used with the sit and down/stay. Repeat this trick two to three times then go back to another trick that Junior already knows. You should never repeat an exercise more than two or three times in succession. Changing things around keeps Junior attentive and prevents him from developing any type of pattern training.

ROLL OVER

The next trick, the roll over, builds on the tummy up. In fact, you are halfway there with the tummy up trick. The hard part is already done. To teach the roll over, keep Junior's head moving all the way around until he has returned his belly to the ground. Be sure to differentiate the two tricks by clearly telling Junior what you want. In the tummy up, the dog should stay when he reaches that position. The roll over has continuous movement from start to finish, without any stay command inserted in between. If you keep it straight, Junior will as well.

CRAWL

The crawling trick is also done from the down/stay position. This must be built on literally one step at a time. Each time Junior makes one move, he must be rewarded.
1. Begin with Junior in a down/stay.

2. Place his target just out of his reach and say, "Junior, crawl."
3. Junior will first stretch his neck, and realizing that he still can't reach his target, he'll reach out with his paw. Praise him and give him his treat.
4. The next time, don't give him the reward until he moves two of his feet, and so on, until he's made an entire four-legged effort to reach his target.

You may need to apply light pressure to his shoulder blades to ensure that he doesn't try to get up and walk to his target. Most dogs will try this. Maintaining the pressure will help Junior understand that he is to remain in his down position while reaching for his target.

Crawling isn't just for toddlers. Puppies can learn how to crawl, too, with the help of a target and lots of praise.

Once you have movement from all four legs, you can increase your criteria to more ground coverage with each crawl request. Within a few training sessions, Junior will be able to crawl at least three to four feet. Gradually, work on increasing your distance from him as you request the behavior. Any time he tries to get up, patiently replace him in his down/stay and back up a bit. Remember that you must often regress in order to progress.

SPINNING AND WEAVING

Spinning around and weaving through your legs is easily taught with your targeting methods. Junior will simply follow his target and gradually associate the commands you use with each exercise. In effect, you are making him successful

This Golden Retriever gets ready to "roll over"—just as soon as he finishes getting his belly scratched.

by offering the same visual cue with each exercise. Through association, Junior will learn the meaning of the word through the repeated action, just as he had learned the meaning of sit. Let's begin with spinning around.

1. Place Junior in a sit/stay and stand in front of him.
2. Show him his target and allow him to follow it in a circle. As you bring his head around say, "Junior, spin." As he moves his body to follow his target, praise him. This will encourage him to continue. When the circle is complete, give him his treat along with more praise.
3. As Junior becomes adept with one circle, add another. Within a short time, Junior will be spinning around and around. He can also begin associating the amount of times you want him to spin by your saying, "Junior, spin three," or "Junior, spin four."

For weaving through your legs, you must also allow Junior to follow your target hand.

1. Spread your legs apart far enough so that Junior can slide through.
2. Show Junior his target from in between your legs. As soon as he gets up to follow the target, praise him.
3. When he makes a complete pass, tell him to sit and give him his treat.

Build on the trick by having Junior follow your target hand around and through your legs before he receives his reward. Next, you can do this trick as you walk. Each time Junior moves through your legs, give him praise, rewarding him with the treat when he completes the trick. The praise will always encourage him to continue, while the reward tells him when the trick is completed.

RETRIEVING

If Junior loves to retrieve, there are many games you and he can play together. The basic ball retrieve only goes so far. A retrieving dog needs a lot of mental stimulation. They can learn to retrieve a specific item, take that item to a specific person (Take-it-to-Harry-game) and perform search and rescue (the Find-It game).

If Junior does not fully understand the idea of retrieving, try the following:
1. Tie a long string to his favorite toy.

Before you begin teaching your puppy new tricks, make sure that he knows how to demonstrate all his basic positions.

If your puppy likes to retrieve, there are many games that you and he can play together.

2. Throw his favorite toy a short distance away. When Junior goes for the toy, praise him.

3. Once Junior has his mouth on the toy, begin drawing it closer to you. Praise Junior as he follows the toy.

4. When you have brought the toy all the way back to you, with Junior either attached or nearby, praise him and give him a reward.

5. Repeat this until Junior learns the pattern of going after the toy and returning to you with the toy for his reward. When you no longer need to bring the toy back with the string, remove it. Junior now retrieves.

Never try to teach your puppy the retrieve by using force. This takes all the fun out of the game and turns it into something he must do or be punished for not doing. This is not a positive approach to training.

Take your time and make sure your puppy enjoys retrieving. Praise and reward him for each little increment of success. Every puppy is different; some may quickly pick up the concept, others may take longer.

Teaching your dog the names of his toys may take a bit of patience and persistence, but it is well worth it. Imagine the fun of asking him to fetch his ball, bone, or stuffed toy and returning to you with it. Once Junior understands the names of the toys, you can hide several of them and ask him to find a specific one. This teaches Junior tracking and discrimination skills, both of which can be used in activities such as obedience trials, search and rescue, substance detection, and field work.

Begin by discovering which toy Junior likes the best through observation

and testing. Try throwing several toys on the floor at the same time. The one he goes to first is his favorite. Teach Junior the name of his toy by repeating it when you tell him to fetch it.

Try throwing two toys— one being his favorite, the other something he rarely shows interest in. If he returns to you with other toys, (however unlikely) send him again. Junior only receives his big reward— your lavish praise and a treat—when he returns to you with the toy you had asked for. Dogs can discriminate between a little reward and a big one. They will always try to get the biggest reward possible. Thus, in using this method, Junior will quickly learn the concept.

Once Junior is regularly retrieving his favorite toy, add a little more difficulty by placing three of his toys a

61

This Golden has the best of both worlds. He gets to play in the water and fetch his favorite toy.

short distance away. Tell him to fetch his favorite. Most likely, he'll return with the one you requested, no matter how many how toys you put in the same location.

The next step is to put away the favorite toy and use his second favorite. Use the same procedures as with the former toy. Junior will be learning the name of his second favorite toy as you proceed to work on this trick. Once he knows the name, it's time to make him really think.

Let's say his favorite toy is a ball and his second favorite a Nylabone®. Place both toys together a short distance away. Ask him first to fetch his ball. When he returns with it, praise him and offer him a reward of some kind. Next, ask him to retrieve the other toy. Always praise him when he returns with the toy.

Put the ball back in its place and ask Junior to fetch his Nylabone® first. If he brings back his ball, ignore him and send him again. At first, he'll be a little confused. After all, he did bring back his favorite toy. Continue to ignore him until he starts to go for the Nylabone®. As soon as he does, praise him. When he returns with the Nylabone®, praise him lavishly and offer him a treat. Continue to mix up which toy you send him for. This teaches Junior to listen for the name of the toy before retrieving it.

This game can be expanded one toy at a time. As Junior learns the names of each toy, there are many different games you can play. Not only does this broaden Junior's mind, it also stimulates your own.

The "take-it" game will give your entire family hours of fun. Begin by asking Junior for a specific toy. When he brings it to you, point to someone, say their name, and tell Junior, "Take it to (place your family member's name here)." That person should ask Junior to come and praise the dog as he nears. As soon as Junior arrives, that person takes the toy, praises the puppy, and gives him a treat. That person then tells Junior to get another toy and who to take it to. That person then calls Junior to come, and so on. Not only are you teaching your dog the different names of his toys, you are also teaching him the names of your family members.

Frisbees™ are a great source of enjoyment for puppies, and it's a game that you can play together.

Games mentally stimulate your puppy as well as provide him with a decent amount of exercise.

to find the next.

Wouldn't it be great if Junior could find your keys or glasses when you lose them? These items can be added to his repertoire as easily as any toy. Junior will enjoy finding whatever object you entreat him to retrieve. Not only will this stimulate his mind, it will also prepare him to be a good service dog, if that is one of your future goals.

Training your puppy can be a huge challenge that includes a lot of hard work and patience. Through positive reinforcement, pet owners can help their puppies enjoy the training process more, while at the same time achieving the desired goals. A puppy is a lifetime commitment that requires love, affection, and guidance. Effective training will ensure that your special puppy grows into a strong, happy, and well-behaved adult dog.

The "find-it" game can also be great fun. Place Junior in a sit or down/stay and place one of his toys a short distance away. Go back to Junior and allow him to see the toy as you send him to fetch it. When he returns with the toy, give him lots of praise and a treat. Repeat this a few times, placing the toy farther and farther away. As Junior becomes adept at fetching the requested toy, begin to hide it halfway behind something. Junior should still be able to see a part of it.

The next step is to completely hide the toy. Tell Junior to find it. He'll put his nose to the ground and search. As soon as he locates the toy, praise him. When he returns to you with it, give him more praise and a treat.

When Junior is able to discriminate which toys are which, you can enhance the game by hiding several of his toys. Ask him to find a specific one. When he returns with that toy, give him his reward then ask him

Once your puppy can successfully retrieve objects and bring them back to you, have him do the same for other members of the family.